ENCINA HIGH SCHOOL
1400 Bell Street
Sacramento, CA 95825
(916) 971-7562
PLEASE RETURN IF FOUND

ENCINA HIGH SCHOOL
1400 Bell Street
Sacramento, CA 95825
(916) 971-7562
PLEASE RETURN IF FOUND

MOVIE MAGIC

MORROW JUNIOR BOOKS   New York

MOVIE MAGIC

Behind the Scenes with Special Effects

ELAINE SCOTT

MORROW JUNIOR BOOKS   New York

MOVIE MAGIC

Acknowledgments

Creating special effects for the movies requires the talent and cooperation of many people. So does writing a book. *Movie Magic* would not exist without the help of those people whose stories I tell in the text, along with many others whose names appear here. I am indebted to each one of these movie magicians, who took time from their busy schedules to share their wisdom and their love of the movies with me so I could pass it on to you. To each of the following people—thank you, thank you.

Halina Krukowski at Lucasfilm Ltd.; Debbie DeNise, Ellen Pasternack, Miles D. V. Perkins, and Ken Ralston at Industrial Light and Magic; Tara Crocitto, Kim Verros, and Stan Winston at Stan Winston Studio; matte artist Jesse Silver; Joe Lombardi and Gabe Videla at Special Effects Unlimited; and Chris, Jeff, and Kevin Yagher at Kevin Yagher Productions.

In addition to all of the above, Marvin Levy and Rebecca Chaires at Amblin Entertainment, Larry McCallister at Paramount Pictures, and Nancy Cushing-Jones at Universal MCA Publishing Rights were invaluable sources of help to me, as were the entire staff at the Margaret Herrick Library at the Center for Motion Picture Study, a division of the Academy of Motion Picture Arts and Sciences, and Terry Geesken at the Museum of Modern Art/Film Stills Archive.

What would I do without the help of editors? Of course I'm grateful to Ellen Dreyer at Morrow Junior Books and Kitty Flynn.

The movies are now one hundred years old. Happy birthday, and may the magic continue!

1 2 3 4 5 6 7 8 9 10

The text type is 12-point Cheltenham.
Book design by Trish Parcell Watts

Library of Congress Cataloging-in-Publication Data
Scott, Elaine.
Movie magic: behind the scenes with special effects/Elaine Scott
p. cm.
Includes index.
ISBN 0-688-12477-1
1. Cinematography—Special effects—Juvenile literature.
[1. Cinematography—Special effects.]   I. Title.
TR858.S36 1995   791.43'024—dc20   95-2166   CIP AC

For my friends Jeanette and Jim Larson, who love books and movies

Contents

The dinosaurs in *Jurassic Park* made film audiences shrink in terror.

Introduction

In darkened movie theaters around the world audiences settle into their seats in eager anticipation as the music swells and the screen lights up. Who knows what thrills or chills await?

From a lovable E.T. to a frightening *T. rex,* fantastic creatures fill the screen in front of us, and for the moment, at least, we believe they are real. Buildings burn, cars crash, people get shot or stabbed, bleed and die—right in front of our horror-stricken eyes! When the show is over, we leave theaters murmuring to ourselves, "I can't believe what I just saw."

Tricks have mystified and entertained audiences since the beginning of civilization. Today, though magicians and their shows remain popular, the most spectacular tricks occur on a movie screen instead of on a stage. And magic wands and incantations have no place in these illusions. Today, art and science have been combined to create the unique magic that, in filmmaking, is called a special effect.

Since the beginning of the movie industry, one hundred years ago, special effects have been used to bring the imagination of the storyteller to life on the screen. By using various clever tricks, special effects artists and technicians have made the unbelievable believable and the impossible possible.

Today's magicians of the movies divide the field of special effects into three general categories—visual effects, physical effects, and makeup effects. Visual effects involve different ways of controlling the cameras and putting a picture together; physical effects (sometimes called mechanical effects) rely on something physical, like a piece of machinery or a miniature puppet, to make the effect happen; and makeup effects are achieved with pots of paint and artificial body parts. Often a combination of effects from more than one category—even from all three—is necessary to achieve the spectacular results that we see on movie screens today.

Today's sophisticated effects demand the talents of artists, model makers, machinists, puppeteers, carpenters, electricians, computer programmers, designers—people with imagination and determination. This book will let you slip behind the scenes and watch these movie magicians at work as they create their illusions and cast their spells.

MOVIE MAGIC

Thomas Edison with George Eastman, the man who invented paper-backed film and a simple box camera that he named Kodak.

The Pioneers

Infant velociraptors emerge from their shells, while a herd of adult raptors runs across a field. Meanwhile, a gentle brachiosaur nibbles the branches of a treetop, and a murderous Tyrannosaurus rex *lurks, waiting to attack anything or anyone that crosses its path. Terrified children and adults are trapped in their car, and audiences watch, horrified, as the attack of the* T. rex *begins.* For the first time in sixty-five million years, dinosaurs have come to life. However, the dinosaurs from *Jurassic Park* were designed and created by humans and computers, not by Mother Nature. This time they dominated a movie screen instead of the world and, in doing so, became one of the movie industry's most spectacular special effects to date.

By comparison to those in *Jurassic Park,* the special effects in the earliest movies were quite crude, though they were created by some of the world's most clever people. Thomas Edison is usually remembered as the man who invented the light bulb and the phonograph. However, in 1891 he applied for a patent for another invention, the kinetoscopic camera. *Kinetic* means "pertaining to motion," and Edison's new camera did just that—it took pictures that moved. People flocked to kinetoscope parlors—forerunners of today's movie theaters—where, one person at a time, they watched the new "movies" in a large rectangular box.

From the very beginning of the movie industry, special effects have been used when it would be impossible, or far too dangerous, to film the real thing. Edison's big hit of 1893 was a one-minute film called *The Execution of Mary,*

Thomas Edison's "execution" of Mary, Queen of Scots, was one of his earliest special effects.

Kinetoscope parlors were the forerunners of today's movie theaters.

Queen of Scots. Viewers paid a nickel each to watch the unfortunate queen lose her head on the chopping block. The movie was filmed at the world's first movie studio, which Edison built near his laboratory in West Orange, New Jersey. Naturally the inventor and his assistant, W.K.L. Dickson (who became the world's first movie director), couldn't find an actress who was willing to part with her head to play the role of Queen Mary, so the two men had to create a special effect. They began by filming an actress on her way to the chopping block, then stopped filming at the moment when the ax was ready to fall. The camera stayed in place and the actress moved away. A look-alike dummy was placed on the executioner's block

Brothers Louis and August Lumière were chemists who invented the *cinématographe,* the first motion-picture projector. Later, the Lumière brothers manufactured photographic plates and paper.

and the filming continued. Down came the ax, and off came the dummy's head! By controlling the film and using a dummy—or model, as filmmakers would say today—Edison was able to achieve the effect he wanted, and one by one, patrons at the kinetoscope parlors were properly horrified as they peered into the boxes to watch the show.

While Edison was working with film in the United States, others were experimenting with it in France. Brothers Louis and August Lumière developed their version of a motion picture camera—one that could project its pictures onto a screen so many people could watch at once. On December 28, 1895 (a date that is frequently given as the official birthday of the movies), the Lumière

brothers showed their films to paying customers at the Grand Café in Paris. A magician, Georges Méliès, was in the audience.

Georges Méliès owned the Théâtre Robert-Houdin, and there he staged his magic shows, performing them against fantastic backgrounds he painted himself. He was called the Magician of Montreuil and was famous throughout France. The Lumière brothers' movies fascinated Méliès, so before long he abandoned his stage act and concentrated on this new form of entertainment.

Georges Méliès is credited with being the first person to raise trick photography to an art form. They say he discovered his first trick quite by accident. One day Méliès was cranking film through his new moving picture camera. He was taking pictures of a bus traveling down a Paris street. The film jammed, but Méliès managed to get it unstuck. He continued to photograph the street traffic. A hearse was passing by, so Méliès filmed that, too. When the film was developed, he was surprised to see that—thanks to the jam in his film—he now had motion pictures of a bus turning into a hearse!

Like Thomas Edison, Méliès had used an effect called stop motion—the act of stopping the film in order to effect a change in the person or thing being photographed. It is a technique that is still used today.

Stop-motion illusions are possible because of the nature of motion picture film. Film is pulled through a movie camera at a constant rate of speed, and the camera usually takes twenty-four pictures, or frames, every single

Georges Méliès is often called the father of trick photography.

second. If you ever look at a piece of movie film, you will see these individual pictures. However, when the film is projected onto a screen at the same speed—twenty-four frames per second—you do not see the split second of darkness that appears after each frame. The pictures seem to blur together as the brain "remembers" the picture it just saw, while it begins to see the new one. This phenomenon is called persistence of vision, and it is present every time you see anything on film.

By discovering that film could be stopped and re-started, Thomas Edison and Georges Méliès paved the way for the special effects used in movies today. Films like *King Kong, The Wizard of Oz,* and, later, *Star Wars* and *Jurassic Park* could never have been made without the pioneering work of Edison and Méliès at the end of the nineteenth century.

At the turn of the century, movies were being made in New York and New Jersey, as well as in France. Few had heard of a small town in California called Hollywood. In 1910, five thousand people lived there. However, its sunny days and interesting landscape of nearby mountains, beaches, and deserts made Hollywood ideal for movie-making. By 1920, thirty-five thousand people called the small town home, and most of the new residents had something to do with the movie industry.

Before long Paramount Pictures, Metro-Goldwyn-Mayer (MGM), Warner Brothers, and 20th Century-Fox, all located in Hollywood, became the most successful and powerful film companies in the world. In the so-called studio

In Georges Méliès's *Cinderella,* stop-motion photography turned the mice into horses and a pumpkin into a coach.

The famous movie creature King Kong began in producer Merian C. Cooper's imagination.

system, each company controlled everything about its movies—including the special effects, which were created at company studios. There was a lot of competition among movie companies, and no studio wanted its technical secrets to get out. It is said that one studio, RKO Radio Pictures, was saved from bankruptcy because of the special effects in one of its films. That 1933 film, *King Kong,* became the *Jurassic Park* of its day, earning a fortune for the studio as people flocked to theaters across the country to see the spectacle of a giant prehistoric gorilla terrorizing New York City in pursuit of the young woman he loved.

King Kong was followed by other spectacular special effects movies, including *The Wizard of Oz,* which MGM released in 1939. Who can forget the scene where the Wicked Witch of the West is melted by a bucket of water? In reality, Margaret Hamilton, who played the witch, stood on a small platform elevator built right into the studio floor. Her long witch's cloak was loosely draped around her shoulders, and its hem was nailed to the wooden floor around the platform. Dry ice was tucked inside the hem of the cloak to make steam. When Dorothy threw the bucket of water, the elevator began its descent, and Margaret Hamilton was lowered right out of her clothes! All that was left of the wicked witch was a pile of steamy black clothing. It was a spectacular mechanical effect for its day.

For various reasons, most of them financial, the studio system has disappeared. Today, many of the big movie companies have sold their California property. Movies are

Margaret Hamilton was lowered out of her costume as she melted away in *The Wizard of Oz*.

made all over the world, and many movie companies rent, rather than own, studio space. Most people working in the movie industry are independent contractors, which means that, from the producer to the actors to the stagehands, each person is hired to work on one specific movie. Once a movie is finished, each person who worked on it goes off to work on a new movie, often at a different studio. It is the same for those who create special effects. Today's movie magicians work independently or with one of several special effects companies that have been created to serve the needs—and imaginations—of moviemakers around the world.

The models and the explosion have been photographed together to make this finished image, called a composite, from *Return of the Jedi*.

A New Generation

The first of the new special effects companies began in 1975. 20th Century-Fox had given a young film director named George Lucas $15,000 to write a screenplay. For three years Lucas worked on his movie story, an exciting and fanciful tale of the future called *Star Wars*. When it was finished, he realized that the film would need new and different kinds of special effects—ones that had never been seen in the movies before. He explained his ideas for these effects to the executives at 20th Century-Fox, and the studio hired him to create them. Lucas assembled a group of young people—some were still teenagers—and put them to work in an industrial warehouse in Van Nuys, California. Among the new employees was a young man named Kenneth Ralston.

When he was just fourteen, Ken and a friend made their first film, *The Bounds of Imagination*. The boys worked in Ken's backyard, using a Kodak home-movie camera and such simple props as a toy snail that appeared to gobble up Ken's finger. "I have always been fascinated with fantasy, science fiction, unusual images," Ken says today.

Ken began his career at age seventeen, building miniatures and making puppets like the Jolly Green Giant and the Pillsbury Doughboy for Cascade Pictures, a film company that produced commercials. Eventually he got tired of making commercials. Ken explains, "Another guy who worked at Cascade, Dennis Muren, was reading a script called *Star Wars*. Dennis and I were ready for a change, and we signed on to work on the film."

Star Wars was the first film Ken Ralston worked on at ILM. Here he shoots a scene with the Blockade Runner.

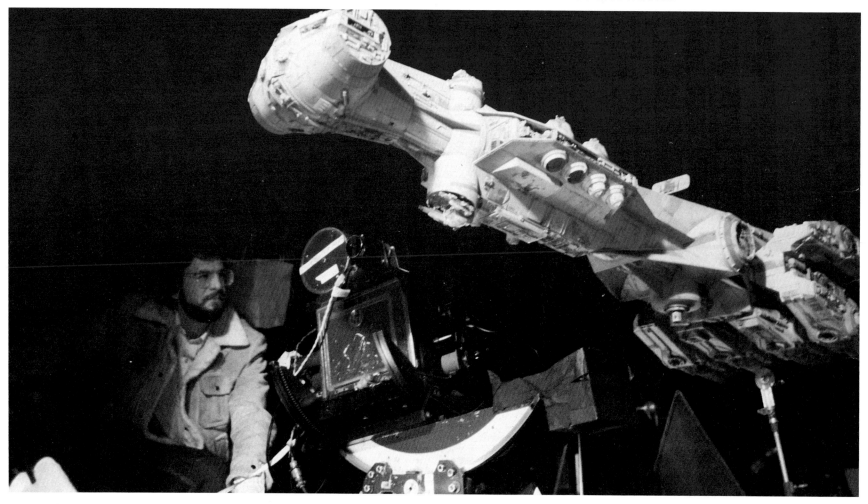

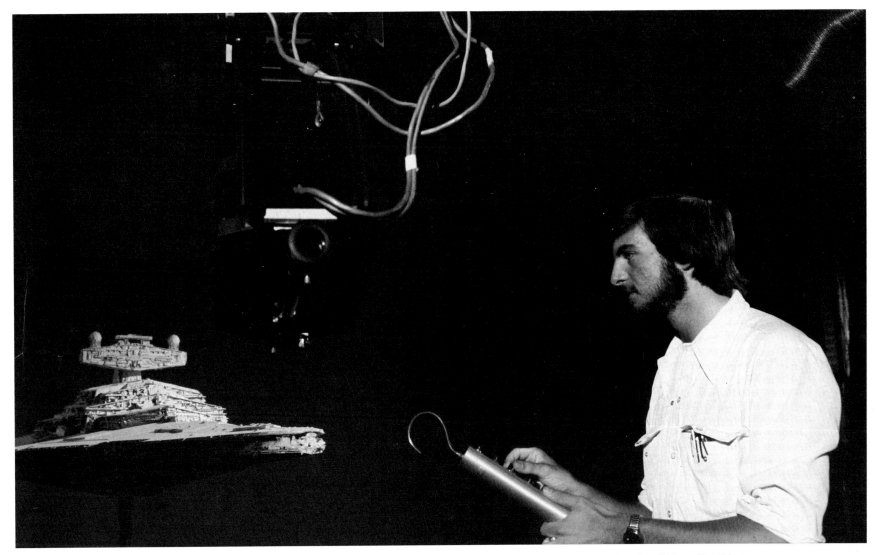

Ken Ralston programs a motion-control camera. The model is a Star Destroyer from the film *The Empire Strikes Back.*

And so Ken Ralston and Dennis Muren, who between them have gone on to win multiple Academy Awards for films like *E.T. The Extra-Terrestrial, Return of the Jedi, Cocoon, Who Framed Roger Rabbit, Terminator 2: Judgment Day, Death Becomes Her,* and *Jurassic Park* (to name just a few), came to join the other young people working at the warehouse in Van Nuys. Although most of them had little experience working in the movies, all of them loved films and understood and could use computers. They called their new company Industrial Light and Magic, or ILM.

These young people were involved with something important that would revolutionize the way special effects were used in the movies. The people at ILM mixed computer technology with the standard special effects techniques Hollywood had been using for years. At ILM, people didn't always control the cameras; computers often did the work. ILM called this new way of filming special effects motion control and used it in *Star Wars* to photograph spaceships streaking across the screen at amazing speeds without any of the jerkiness that would be seen if a human were running the camera.

By using computers, the wizards at ILM discovered they could also add depth and details to a scene. In addition to producing a steady picture, the computer-controlled camera could repeat a shot again and again with absolute precision. Therefore, ILM could photograph the same spaceship many times, adding details like engine glows and running lights with each new pass of the camera. When the pictures were layered together like a sandwich, the final results were more realistic than anything movie audiences had seen before. In the opening scene of *Star Wars* a spaceship looms realistically in the sky overhead, and there are stories that audiences, surprised by what they saw, burst into spontaneous applause. Special effects are *supposed* to surprise the audience, but as with

any good surprise, a new and different special effect takes time and patience to plan and create.

Just as there are various kinds of special effects, there are various types of special effects companies to execute them. Some are small and specialize in only one kind of effect—lightning, for example, or fiery explosions. Other companies are large, like ILM, and are able to produce all the effects that might be needed for a feature film.

Ken Ralston began his career at ILM in 1975, working as a camera assistant on *Star Wars*. Almost twenty years later, after numerous Academy Awards, when the opening credits of *Forrest Gump* ran in theaters, Ken Ralston's name appeared alone on the screen as the film's special effects supervisor. Like an orchestra with a conductor, a film needs one person—the FX (filmmakers' shorthand for the word *effects*) supervisor—to coordinate the talents of many people and bring them together to work on a film. Ken describes his job by saying, "My favorite part is in the beginning, when anything goes. Ideas are flowing, and I'm like a magician pulling something out of a hat. I read the script, get together with the director, and help design the special effects shots that he or she requires."

Planning for a special effect begins by boarding the shot—illustrating key moments of action in a series of sketches called a storyboard. Some people say that storyboards originated in the 1930s at the Walt Disney studio. Artists there would make rough sketches of each scene in a cartoon, then pin their sketches on a bulletin board. Since many artists worked on each cartoon, having a

FORREST GUMP Shot Information Sheet — 1/10/94

DESCRIPTION:
Forrest puts his son on the bus, the feather floats up.

SHOT #: 275/1

STORYBOARD:

COMP TYPE:	SHOT LENGTH:	PLATE SHOOT DATE:	CUT INFO DUE:
CG	1079X	9/17/93	Received 12/22/93

PRODUCTION ELEMENTS:	POST PRODUCTION ELEMENTS:
BG Plate	Feather (Bluescreen) Feather G-Matte (CG)

NOTES/EQUIPMENT:

The floating-feather sequence from *Forrest Gump* was sketched on a storyboard before filming ever began.

series of sketches on a board functioned a bit like a road map: The sketches helped all the artists follow the same story line. Others say that storyboards, or production sketches, began with Georges Méliès, the French magician and artist. Méliès always sketched a scene he was going to film before he did anything else.

A storyboard works a little like the outline you might make before you write a paper. An outline helps you plan exactly what you are going to include in your paper; in a way, it helps you "see" your paper before you write it. In a similar way, a storyboard helps the effects technicians see what they are supposed to do with a particular effect. A storyboard includes information about the camera, whether it will be pulled back or up close. The storyboard will also show the POV, or point of view. Who is seeing the action? Is the audience watching the characters respond to the action, or has the camera *become* one of the actors, so the audience can watch the scene as the character would see it? All of these things must be considered when special effects are planned, so storyboards are indispensable in special effects filmmaking.

Sometimes a director will want something more than a storyboard to help visualize effects. If a movie includes monsters, dragons, or other strange creatures that exist only in a writer's imagination, the director may ask to see a sketch, called a conceptual design, of the creature. But a sketch is often not enough for a director; he or she might need more help to be able to visualize the final creature. Ken Ralston says that small sculptures or models, called

A carefully rendered pencil drawing—such as this of the gigantic *T. rex* from *Jurassic Park*—can show a director the way a special effects creature might look in action.

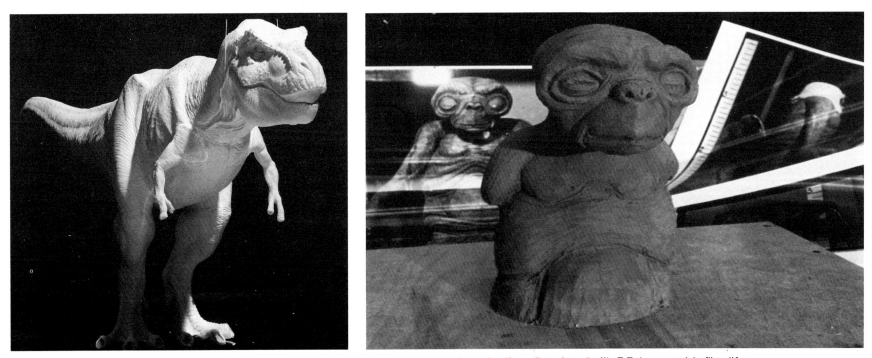

After the drawing stage, a maquette, or model, helps flesh out the creature for the director *(left)*. E.T. began his film life as a model *(right)*.

maquettes, are often the best way to sell an idea to a director, and Ken frequently creates more than one version of the same creature in maquette form. "We ask the director what he likes, or doesn't like, about each one," Ken says. "We are creating the illusion of what these impossible things could be."

Once everyone knows what special effects will be needed for a shot, and the shot is boarded, it is broken up into its different elements—something called a shot breakdown. There are good reasons for doing shot breakdowns. First, it helps the FX supervisor see how the final effect will actually work, and second, it helps the special effects company creating the shot decide how much it will cost. For example, in *Forrest Gump,* the floating feather that lands on Tom Hanks's foot at the beginning of the film and floats away at the end took months to plan before it was filmed. Later in this book you will read more about how that shot was created.

The special effects that make today's movies fun to watch are carefully planned—and very expensive—illusions.

Kevin Yagher poses with some of the monsters he has created.

Making Monsters

Kevin Yagher, president of Kevin Yagher Productions, and his brother, Jeff, grew up loving monster magazines. "Jeff started before me, spending his allowance on them. I saved my money and just read his," says Kevin.

"We were always sculpting things and making masks. We used things from around the house—scraps of cloth for costumes, bread-dough clay for monster teeth." As Kevin tells the story, the boys once got into trouble with their hobby. Jeff had designed some very realistic werewolf masks. He and Kevin went out one night wearing them, and, in a field near their home, they acted out a story they had made up. Unfortunately, their masks and costumes must have been too realistic—when a neighbor spotted the boys, he called the police. From then on, when the Yagher boys wore their monster masks, they stuck to their own backyard!

Jeff and Kevin's boyhood interest in monsters, makeup, and acting lives on.

As a teenager, Jeff Yagher perfected his werewolf makeup.

Jeff decided he liked acting more than monster making. Kevin, on the other hand, continued to love sculpting and drawing. Today, this Emmy Award–winning young man is president of an effects company that specializes in creating animated puppets and special makeup effects for movies and television. Walk into his warehouse and you will be greeted by images of Freddy Krueger, from the *Nightmare on Elm Street* movies, and the Crypt Keeper, from television's "Tales from the Crypt," along with the far-less-frightening seven-foot-tall baby used in *Honey, I Blew Up the Kid.*

"It's all about creating an illusion," Kevin says as he points to the body forms and molds, piles of hair and eyeballs, arms and legs, tiny motors, and rolls of masking tape that fill his warehouse in a suburb of Los Angeles.

Kevin and his crew dip into these supplies regularly to fashion his creatures.

The artists and technicians at Kevin Yagher Productions can build any kind of realistic or fantastic creature a director might want. For the film *Bill & Ted's Bogus Journey,* Kevin was asked to build an imaginary

Extra parts for the Crypt Keeper are stored in a box at Kevin Yagher's studio.

30

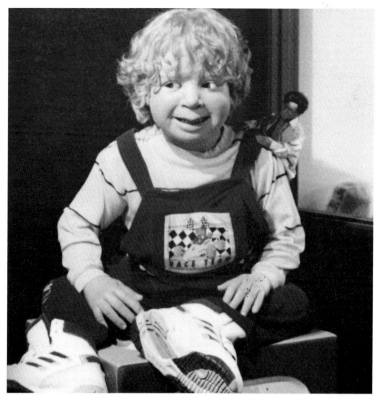

Two of Kevin Yagher's creatures—Freddy Krueger *(above)* and the giant "kid" *(above right)*. First the skull, then the motors, then the final mechanized head for the kid in *Honey, I Blew Up the Kid (right)*.

creature called Station. Once the conceptual design and the maquette were approved, Kevin and his team began to build the puppet. A puppet begins with an armature, or skeleton, made from carefully machined metal parts. The armature's various pieces are joined so the puppet will be able to bend and move easily—a process called articulation. The more articulated, or movable, a puppet is, the more realistic it will appear on the screen. Station had a fully articulated armature, one that moved all parts of the puppet's body. Station's body, like the bodies of most other movie puppets, was created by the following process.

Using the design sketch as a guide, Kevin and his assistants first sculpted Station's body out of clay, putting in all the details from the original sketch. When the clay sculpture was just as Kevin wanted it, the team was ready to cast the mold. The mold would take the shape of the Station sculpture, but it would be just the opposite of it. Model makers call this a negative mold. If you have ever had a cast on an arm or leg and looked at it when it was removed, you may have noticed that you had a negative mold of your body part.

The mold for Station, like most puppet molds, was made in two castings, front and back. The sculpture was divided by pressing a clay product completely around and halfway up one side of the sculpture. A marble was pressed into the clay to serve as an impression key, a kind of peg that would allow the two halves of the mold to be aligned perfectly when it was time to cast the actual puppet.

The creature called Station is sculpted out of clay.

The mold for Station was huge. When it was finished, it was used to create the creature's musculature, which was made out of fiberglass. Fiberglass "muscles" protected the metal armature and provided a foundation for Station's latex "skin." To make the skin, Kevin poured liquid foam latex into the mold, and the entire thing was baked until the foam rubber cured, or hardened, into a solid substance. The skin was fitted over the fiberglass form and painted; then individual horsehairs were attached, one by one, with a needle.

Individual horsehairs were attached by hand.

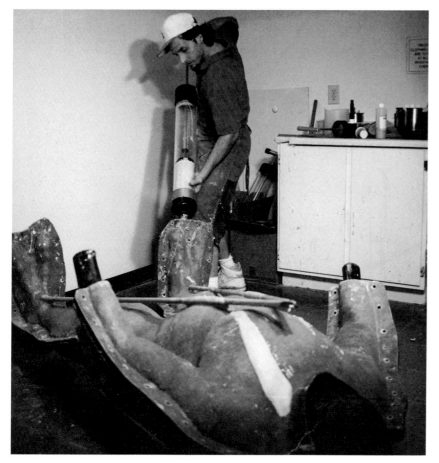

Foam rubber is injected into the giant Station mold.

Next a special kind of plaster called Ultracal was poured over the exposed half of the sculpture and allowed to harden. When the first half was hard enough, the clay was removed from the second half of the sculpture and the process was repeated. Finally, there were two casts, or molds—one of the front and one of the back of the puppet.

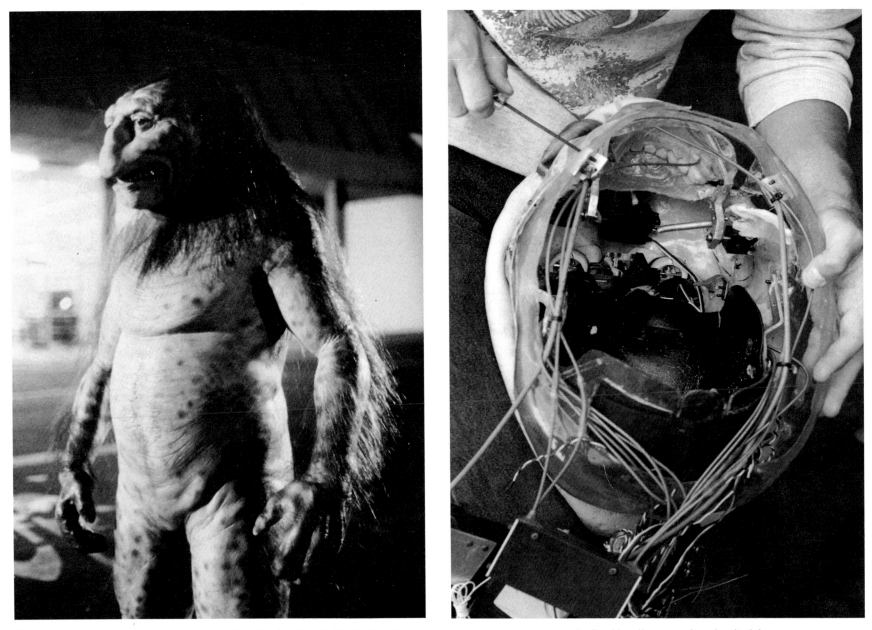

Final details were spray painted on Station's skin *(left)*. Station's facial expressions were controlled by the mechanics inside the skull *(right)*.

But of course skin and bones are not the only things that make up a realistic puppet. Creatures—real or imaginary—have muscles that move and eyes that roll and a mouth that smiles, frowns, growls, or roars. Beneath the latex flesh, Kevin placed tiny motors wherever he thought Station needed movement. Puppeteers controlled the movement by cables attached to these motors. The movie called for several creatures like Station, and Kevin Yagher's studio built each one

Station had to be believable, but it didn't have to be realistic; for *Jurassic Park,* however, Stan Winston and the artists at his special effects company, Stan Winston Studio, were asked to design and create dinosaurs that were believable *and* realistic. Stan discussed creating the dinosaurs, saying, "It all begins with the art—the art gives you the essence of the character. Before you can do anything technically, you have to know what the creature will look like, how you want it to perform. The art always comes before the technology."

The art was created by Stan Winston's concept artist, Mark "Crash" McCreery. Crash began by studying the work of paleontologists to be certain that his drawings would reflect the latest understanding about these prehistoric creatures. Next, using an artist's pencil, he created detailed drawings, which were sent to *Jurassic Park*'s director, Steven Spielberg, for approval. Once the approval came, other artists at Winston's studio made copies of Crash's drawings and painted them with different combinations of colors. This artwork also went to

Stan Winston poses with some of the monsters he has created.

35

RANNOSAURUS REX, STAN WINSTON STUDIO

Crash McCreery's concept drawing for the *T. rex.*

Spielberg, who made the final decision about the coloring the creatures would have. "We spent a great deal of time studying the truth," Stan Winston says. "Then we put our instincts and artistic skills together to create what we feel are real dinosaurs."

Stan's team created two models of the *T. rex* before they built the final nine-thousand-pound, twenty-five-foot-tall creature. The smallest model was built to 1/16 scale. "We sent that one to Phil Tippett at ILM, who created an armature for it," Stan says. "Phil had to answer the questions about how the various dinosaurs acted—how they walked, how they ran. He played with the small model

The giant dinosaur was created first as a 1/5-scale model *(foreground),* then as a full-scale sculpture *(background).*

much like someone plays with a motion figure toy, until he created the look of the performance of the dinosaurs."

Once Phil decided how the dinosaurs would look in action, he created their performance "bible"—a book that everyone on the film referred to when they had questions about how the dinosaurs should look when they moved.

Next Stan built the armatures for the 1/5-scale model and the final, gigantic *T. rex.* "We had mechanical engineers involved who understand stress and weight and thrust," he says. "We also used people who had been involved in amusement park characters and rides—people who understood the concept of 'big.' But we had to

The armature, or skeleton, for the giant *T. rex* from *Jurassic Park* was controlled by a hydraulic system similar to those used in flight simulators.

come up with a dinosaur that didn't look like it came out of an amusement park. We wanted something that moved smoothly and looked and acted real."

Stan used hydraulics—a system that uses the force of water or other liquids to run a machine—and telemetry—the process of carrying electrical impulses from one location to another—to move his massive *T. rex*. The dinosaur's body was mounted on top of the hydraulic system. Since that dinosaur was far too large to be moved by people, the smaller version was used instead. Puppeteers moved its head, neck, and body, and those movements were carried by telemetry to the big puppet, which duplicated every move. "These creatures had to act," Stan comments. "They had to change their performance from

For some scenes, the attack of the *T. rex* was controlled by a computer.

shot to shot and do whatever Steven Spielberg wanted them to do at that point." The telemetry system allowed the dinosaurs to respond as living creatures, not amusement park attractions—whose repeated movements are often stiff and unbelievable.

However, there were times when Stan and Steven Spielberg wanted the *T. rex* to repeat movements exactly,

take after take. To do that, the dinosaur's hydraulic system was interfaced into a computer system. There is a scene in the film where the enraged *T. rex* pushes Malcolm, the character played by actor Jeff Goldblum, through a restroom wall. The wall was a breakaway, meaning it was built to break easily in a certain spot. The mechanical monster needed to move precisely and push

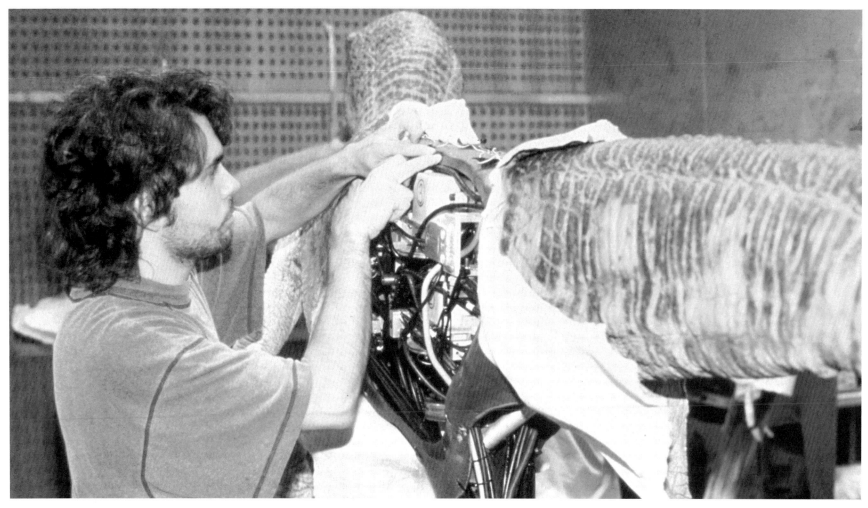

At Stan Winston's studio, an artist fits the velociraptor armature with its skin.

the actor through the wall in the right place. The movement of the giant head and the distances it traveled were carefully planned and measured. Then those figures were entered into the computer that controlled the *T. rex.* When the moment came, a button was pushed and the *T. rex* crashed its face—and the stunt actor who stood in for Jeff Goldblum—through the soft spot in the wall, exactly as planned. Stan says, "We could program the *T. rex* to hit exactly the same spot over and over again. It was a big, scary nine-thousand-pound creature that could have killed someone, so the computer system also provided an element of safety."

Computers and telemetry, cables and hydraulics are not the only way to control the movement of a special effects puppet. Occasionally, human beings occupy the foam latex skin and control the puppet by using their bodies, with additional movements supplied by cables and motors. Human beings wore velociraptor "suits" in some scenes in *Jurassic Park,* and the Crypt Keeper in "Tales from the Crypt" is often controlled by a small person inside the Crypt Keeper costume.

No matter how they are moved, creatures have always played important roles in the movies. Stan Winston says about his dinosaurs, "We wanted the audience to experience real dinosaurs as they walked the earth—what they really were, what they really looked like, how they really acted—and not think of them as a special effect."

With each succeeding year, puppets of creatures both real and imaginary become more believable, as computer science and artistic talent come together to bring them to life.

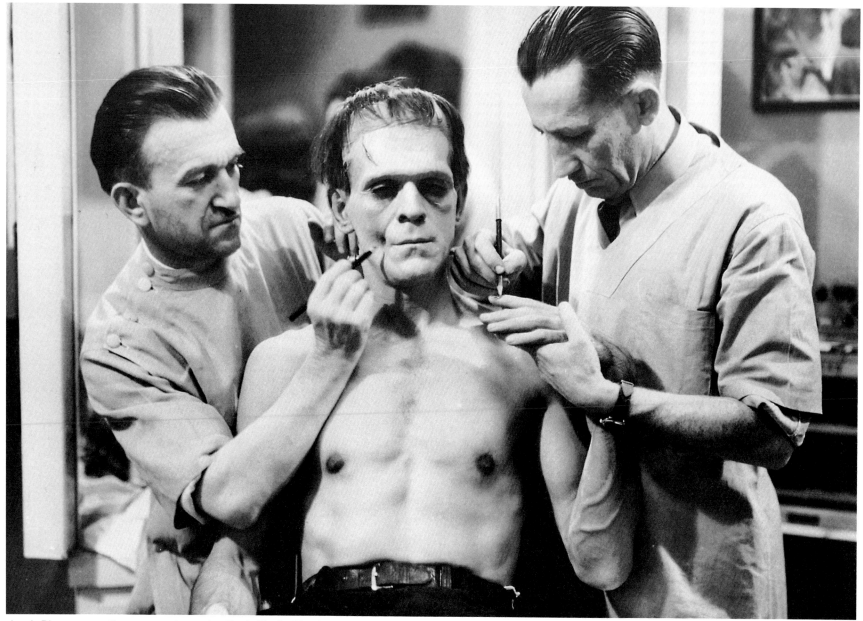

Jack Pierce applies a scar to actor Boris Karloff's cheek, while another makeup artist applies black fingernail polish to Dr. Frankenstein's classic monster.

Making Up

The Man of a Thousand Faces was a nickname for silent-screen actor Lon Chaney, who was famous for his portrayals of monstrous beings in such early films as *The Hunchback of Notre Dame* (1923) and *The Phantom of the Opera* (1925). Lon Chaney invented nearly all of his special makeup effects himself, and he carefully guarded the secrets. He was also willing to endure excruciating pain while wearing some of the makeup. In one movie, he played a blind man, and in order to give his eye a cloudy effect, he covered it with the lining of an eggshell. In *The Hunchback of Notre Dame,* the actor relied on manipulating his own body to achieve some of his most grotesque effects. Though he never discussed it, it appears that he pulled up his nose and pinned back his ears before applying the makeup for that film. There have been revivals of *The Phantom of the Opera* on Broadway and in the movies, but most critics still say that Lon Chaney's portrayal of the strange masked man who haunted the Paris Opera House was the most frightening one of all.

Actor Lon Chaney in makeup as the Phantom in *The Phantom of the Opera.*

clever use of makeup and a little studying on his own. "I discovered there are six ways a surgeon can cut the skull," he later said, "and I figured Dr. Frankenstein, who was not a practicing surgeon, would take the easiest. That is, he would cut the top of the skull straight across like a pot lid, hinge it, pop the brain in, and clamp it tight. That's the reason I decided to make the monster's head square and flat like a box." In order to achieve this effect, Pierce built a prosthesis, or artificial body part, to fit the top of Boris Karloff's head, giving it a square, boxlike look. Pierce topped off the prosthesis with a wig, and the rest of the illusion was completed with makeup. The makeup was so unique that it was protected by a copyright and could not be duplicated without permission from the studio.

The original versions of *Frankenstein, Dracula,* and *The Phantom of the Opera* were all filmed in black-and-white, and makeup artists took that into consideration when they were concocting their effects. For example, Boris Karloff's makeup in *Frankenstein* was really a blue-green face paint. This paint would not work for a color movie today, but on black-and-white film, it photographed as a sickly white. In early films, chocolate syrup was often used as blood for the same reason—it photographed more realistically than a red substance.

Thomas Edison made the first Frankenstein movie in 1910, but the classic monster of the screen, who has been imitated but never surpassed, is the monster portrayed by actor Boris Karloff in the 1931 horror movie *Frankenstein.* Makeup artist Jack Pierce turned the mild-mannered Karloff into Dr. Frankenstein's monster by

The fake blood used in today's films is often made from a mixture of red coloring and corn syrup. If a movie is going to be particularly gory, the blood can be mixed with pieces of fake flesh. Some directors can get quite bloodthirsty in their quest for realism!

Makeup can be used to simulate wounds, but it is also used to change actors into other kinds of creatures. Boris Karloff wore a relatively simple prosthesis to play the part of Dr. Frankenstein's monster. Makeup artist John Chambers designed far more elaborate ones for the film *Planet of the Apes.* This movie tells the story of a future Earth ruled by apes instead of humans. The "apes" in the movie bear an eerie resemblance to human beings. However, ape faces and human faces, while similar in structure, are certainly not alike. The ape faces were shaped with special prostheses made out of rubber and attached to the actors' faces. More of this specially mixed rubber compound was molded to their features, allowing the actors to talk and move their lips naturally. Because the nose of an ape sits far higher on its face than a human nose does, the actors who wore the ape makeup actually breathed through a small passage in the mask's upper lip.

Since this elaborate makeup took at least three hours to apply, there was no time to take it off and put it back on during the day. In order to eat lunch, the actors used mirrors to locate their mouths. Checking in the mirror, they pushed their food, cut into small bites, through their outer ape lips and into their real mouths. Although the ape makeup was not painful, as Lon Chaney's often was, it had to be endured during a blazing Arizona summer when the temperatures outside reached 120 degrees.

Ape makeup from *Planet of the Apes* took hours to apply and was difficult to wear.

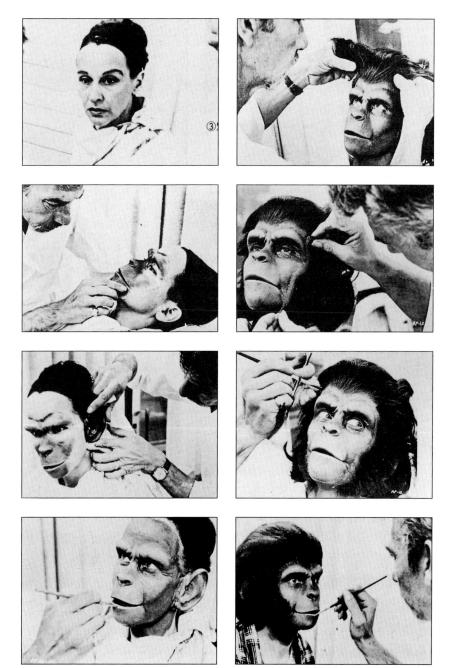

45

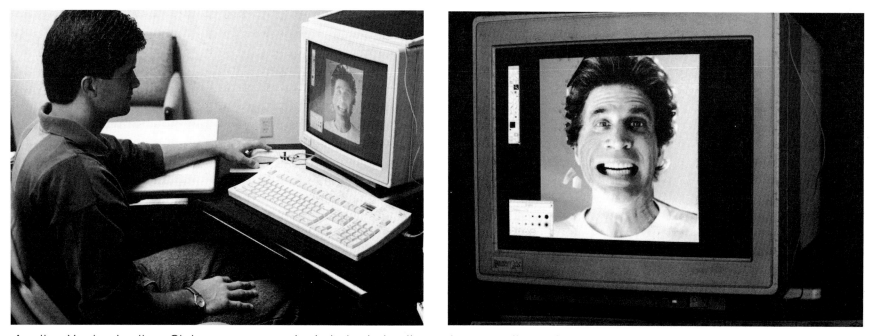

Another Yagher brother, Chris, uses a computer to help design the makeup prostheses for actor Ted Danson to wear *(left)*. A computer can stretch a smile to an impossible width *(right)*!

Special effects makeup often uses prostheses to turn people into apes or werewolves or to achieve looks that simply aren't found in real life. Although most makeup artists sketch or sculpt the looks they want as they plan their effects, today computers also help makeup artists.

In the film *Getting Even with Dad,* actors Ted Danson and Macaulay Culkin had a scene in which they rode on a roller coaster with the ominous name G-Force. Kevin Yagher was asked to create makeup for Danson and Culkin that would make it look as if their faces were almost blowing off. Kevin first studied photographs of objects in wind tunnels to see how great wind forces affect things. Then he took pictures of Ted Danson and Macaulay Culkin and scanned them into a computer. With the photos in the computer, Kevin was able to move the actors' mouths and cheeks around, stretching them back as far as he wanted—much farther than they could possibly stretch in real life! When he was satisfied with the look, Kevin asked the actors to sit for molds of their faces.

After putting straws in the actors' nostrils to help them breathe, Kevin carefully spread special plaster over their faces and let it dry into molds. He used these molds to create clay models of their faces that he could then sculpt to match the expressions he had created in the computer.

46

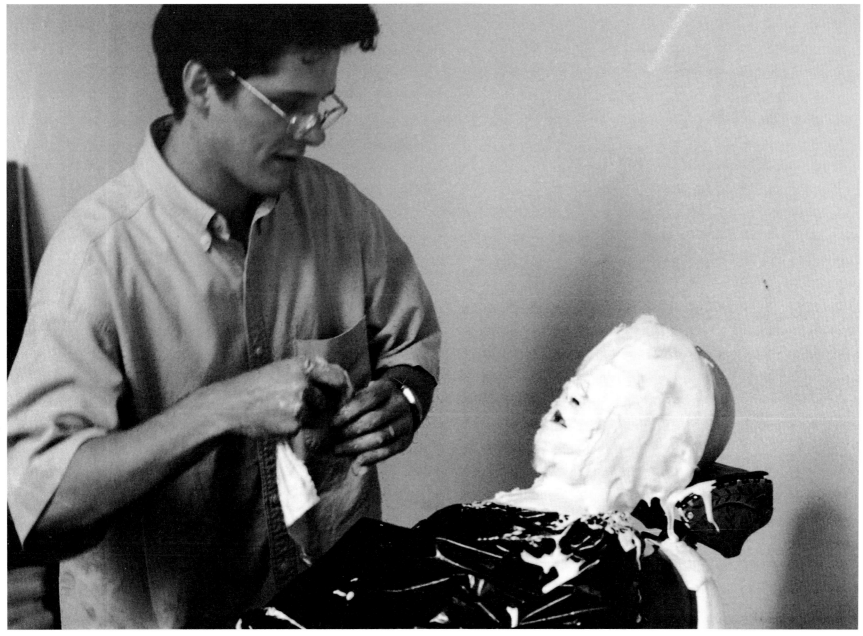

Kevin Yagher takes a mold of Macaulay Culkin's face.

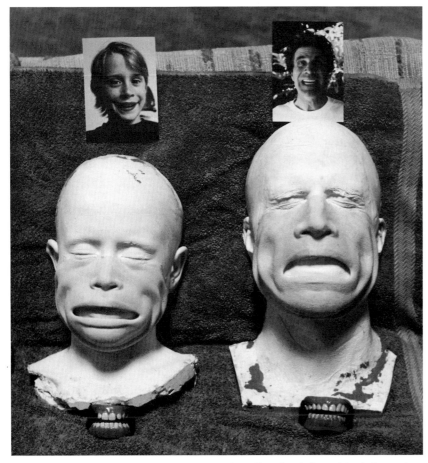

Foam prostheses are carefully fitted to the facial molds *(above)*. When the foam is cured, the prosthesis is carefully removed from the mold *(right)*.

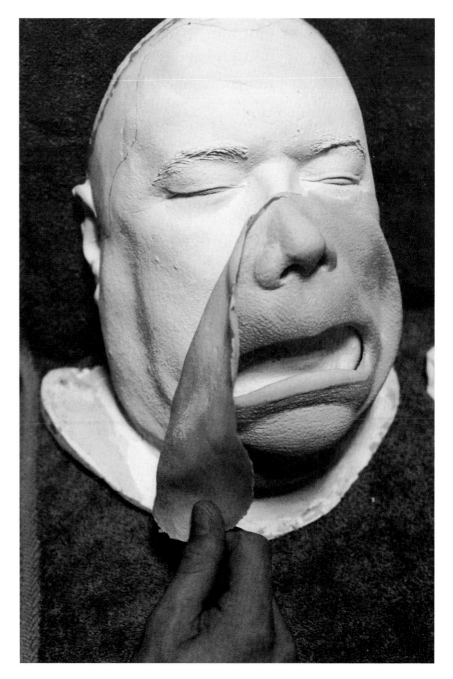

When Kevin had each head sculpted the way he wanted it to look on the roller coaster, he took a new mold from that sculpture, poured in the foam, and took off the prosthesis that became the actor's "new" cheeks and mouth. Scenes in movies are often shot more than once

48

before they are just right, so since these prostheses were thin and delicate and could easily rip, Kevin made several sets.

Movie makeup today has evolved from the powder, lipstick, and eye pencils of the earliest films into a true art form that uses high-tech tools and requires the ability to design and execute many different looks. In recognition of the contribution that clever makeup adds to a film, the Academy of Motion Picture Arts and Sciences has instituted a special Oscar for makeup, one that is not necessarily awarded each year. The 1993 Academy Award for makeup went to the talented artists who changed Robin Williams's appearance from male to female in the hit film *Mrs. Doubtfire*.

The makeup that turned Robin Williams into Mrs. Doubtfire won an Academy Award for makeup artists Greg Cannom, Ve Neill, and Yolanda Toussieng.

Stunt actors race across the burning set during filming of *Gone With the Wind*.

Fire, Wind, and Rain

Gone With the Wind was released in 1939, and audiences around the world flocked to see it. In one classic scene in the film, the city of Atlanta burns while Rhett Butler and Scarlett O'Hara escape in a horse-drawn wagon. The effect was realistic, and things *were* on fire, but of course the real city of Atlanta was perfectly safe. The burning took place on the back lot of the MGM studios on December 10, 1938, while executives and invited guests gathered to watch the blaze in a partylike atmosphere. Many sets from previous MGM movies— including a tall wooden wall from *King Kong*—had been painted to represent Atlanta. At the proper moment, a fire was lit. Thousands of gallons of fuel were pumped in to feed it, and the flames leaped upward. The studio did not want to risk the safety of the movie's two stars, so stunt actors representing Scarlett and Rhett drove across the fiery set in a horse-drawn wagon. The camera, the stunt actors, the horse, the wagon, and the fire had to work perfectly the first time, because if anything at all had gone wrong with that shot, it could not have been repeated. In six minutes the shot was over, and the entire set was burned to ashes. Fortunately nothing went wrong, and when you watch that movie today the effect of the fire is still spectacular.

Fire is an unpredictable element, and moviemakers continue to use it with great caution. At the time of its release, *Backdraft* took the record for the most extensive use of fire in a film. *Backdraft*'s director, Ron Howard, wanted to tell a story about real fire fighters, and he wanted to show audiences, as closely as possible, what it was like to be inside a blazing inferno. The challenge was great—create a film that looked dangerous while keeping everyone associated with it safe.

The most spectacular scene in *Backdraft*—something moviemakers often call the payoff shot—occurs near the end of the film, when fire fighters run across the roof of a blazing building as it collapses behind them. No one was going to set a real building on fire, so a full-scale model of a building was constructed and set up on an unused railroad bridge over a highway in Los Angeles. Burners, similar in principle to the burners on a gas stove, were placed underneath the model.

Clay Pinney, the movie's FX director, designed the burners for *Backdraft*. They were pipes with special slits cut into them to allow the fuel to escape and be lit. Even the fuel was carefully selected: Clay chose diesel fuel because it produces more haze than smoke when it burns. Too much smoke would make it impossible for the audience to see the fire fighters running in the middle of the

blaze. When the fire was lit and the scene was shot, the stunt actors playing the fire fighters had to be extremely careful as they ran across the burning roof. One false step and they could have fallen onto the burners below.

In another spectacular bit of film trickery for *Backdraft*, a movie camera was fitted with special tiles, exactly like those that cover the space shuttles and protect them from the heat of the fiery reentry into Earth's atmosphere. The protected camera was set in place, and as the fire blazed around it, the camera rolled. From this point of view, the camera *became* the fire fighters, so the resulting image made audiences sense what it is like to be trapped inside a raging inferno.

It is one thing to set a building on fire in the movies. It is another to set people on fire. Stunt actors do this kind of dangerous work, and their lives depend on the expertise of special effects technicians who know exactly what they are doing when they work with fire. In all movies that have human torches in them, the stunt actors first put on tight-fitting protective fire suits beneath their other clothing. The fire suits allow the actors to withstand the heat of a fire for at least one minute, which is a *long* time when flames are licking at your back! Since fire eats up oxygen quickly, and the actors must be able to breathe during their effects shot, small canisters of oxygen are tucked into the fire suits. There is usually enough air in these canisters to last about three minutes. Another suit, this one made of asbestos, goes over the fire suit, and a protective hood is put in place over the actor's head and face. If the

Backdraft contained some of the most realistic fire scenes ever filmed.

camera is going to take a close shot, the stunt actor might wear a fireproof mask, sculpted to resemble the actor whose place he or she is taking, over the fireproof hood.

Pyrotechnics can add a lot of realism and excitement to a movie, but it can add tension, too. Ron Howard described *Backdraft* as "a dangerous movie to make. I lost

53

sleep over it . . . and I only relaxed when it was finished." Nevertheless, the fire effects in that film were so spectacular that Clay Pinney won an Academy Award.

"Action is a major part of filmmaking," says Gabe Videla, a partner in Special Effects Unlimited. "Audiences—especially young people—like movies where good is pitted against evil." In an action movie, the battle of good against evil usually does involve some kind of fire—it may be a blast from a gun, an exploding bomb, or a full-scale simulated war.

Gabe's partner at Special Effects Unlimited, Joe Lombardi, founded the company in 1946. Soon after, he became the FX supervisor for the "I Love Lucy" television program. Today, however, Joe and Gabe's firm specializes in mechanical and environmental special effects, and a lot of their work involves weapons, fire, wind, and rain.

Wind is relatively easy to generate on a movie set. In most cases, giant fans will do the trick. However, tornadoes and other kinds of winds can be difficult to fake. Back in 1939, Arnold Gillespie, the FX supervisor for *The Wizard of Oz,* had to create the illusion of the tornado that carried Dorothy and Toto to Oz. He solved his problem by using a fan to blow air through a silk stocking!

Inside a studio filled with "rain," Gene Kelly danced during a scene from *Singin' in the Rain (above right).* The tornado in *The Wizard of Oz* was actually a woman's stocking *(right).*

Water effects range from easy to ingenious, and smoke can be created with machines or a combination of chemicals. Rain is relatively easy to duplicate. If the movie company is filming inside, pipes with holes in them are suspended over the rainy area. Then water is pumped through these pipes, and fans scatter the drops as they fall. Depending on the volume of water and the speed of the fans, technicians can create an illusion of gentle April showers or a full-blown hurricane. Outdoors, effects artists will often use fire hoses spraying up into the air, also with fans to scatter the drops of water as they fall.

When a scene requires large amounts of water, effects artists use water tanks and dump tanks to provide it. A dump tank is a bit like a dump truck. The tank can be tilted, so the water pours out in a rush. In 1923, Cecil B. DeMille had to re-create the biblical miracle of Moses parting the Red Sea for his movie *The Ten Commandments*. In order to achieve the effect, DeMille did not wait for divine intervention. Instead he called on the talents of Paramount Pictures FX supervisors Fred Moran and Roy Pomeroy. Moran and Pomeroy "parted" the Red Sea by using a dump tank to pour water into a specially constructed U-shaped trough. When the film of this shot was run backward, it looked as if the waters were being parted. Keeping the waters apart so the Israelites could cross was another problem. Pomeroy solved it by making

At Special Effects Unlimited, rain is created by pumping water through vertical rain towers *(left)*. An umbrella protects Gabe Videla from the tower's drizzle *(center)*. From drizzle to downpour, this artificial rain is still wet!

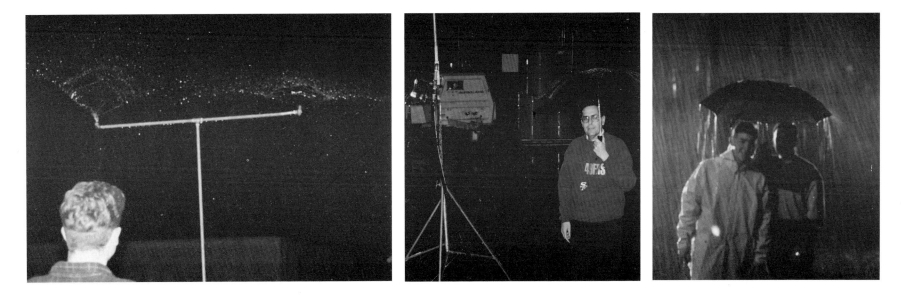

Joe Lombardi planned this fire effect for *The Flight of the Intruder.*

The Cuyahoga River "burning" made the front page of the *Cleveland Plain Dealer.*

some Jell-O, which he then cut in half. Now he had two quivering masses that, when photographed properly, looked surprisingly like shimmering walls of water. He also took live-action footage of the actors as they fled from Pharaoh's armies. This piece of film was inserted into the Jell-O footage, and the effect was convincing enough for its time.

Sometimes water and fire elements are combined for an exciting shot. For a 1994 movie called *Double Dragon*, Joe Lombardi set the Cuyahoga River in Cleveland, Ohio, on fire. He and his crew of hand-chosen special effects technicians carefully laid miles of perforated pipe in a trench they dug underneath the river. Propane gas was pumped through the pipes. The scene called for planes to fly overhead and bomb the river. At precisely the right time, on a signal from Joe and his crew, the propane was ignited and the Cuyahoga River burst into flame. The entire scene made the Cleveland nightly television news. The river still flows peacefully, and Joe proudly says, "I didn't even singe a tree."

Bullet hits effectively scarred the car and the actors in the death scene from *Bonnie and Clyde*.

Help! I'm Wounded!

If you were to watch Edison's film about the beheading of Mary, Queen of Scots, it would be pretty obvious that no one parted with a head on that chopping block. But in Roman Polanski's 1971 film version of Shakespeare's *Macbeth,* the actor playing the title role lost his head, and this time the camera showed the entire gory event. Of course, no one was really beheaded then, either. In *Macbeth* the effect was achieved with fake blood, models, and an actor inside a full suit of armor. The top of the armor was outfitted with an artificial head and neck, with a good supply of fake blood. The camera began filming and continued as the artificial head was chopped off the body. Blood splattered everywhere. As the head fell to the bottom of the scaffold, the camera cut to a shot of Jon Finch, the actor who played Macbeth. His head appeared to be lying in a pool of blood on the ground, but in reality, the "ground" was a raised platform through which the actor had poked his head. It is an effective shot. Some might even say it is too realistic.

Actors have been getting shot and stabbed since the earliest days of the movie industry. In the beginning, sharpshooters were hired to fire guns with live ammunition at very nervous actors, aiming only inches away from them! No one uses this method anymore. People are still "shot," but the bullets and blood are not real. With a slight smile on his face, Joe Lombardi says, "I've shot a lot of people in my day, and I haven't hurt any of them."

However, the truth is that even though guns in movies always fire blanks instead of bullets, even a blank can be dangerous. A blank is a cartridge that has been plugged where the bullet would be, then crimped shut. When a gun is fired, moviegoers see the flash from its barrel and the smoke. The amount of flash and smoke is controlled by the amount of gunpowder loaded into the blanks. FX supervisors talk about blanks having quarter, half, or full loads, or charges, in them. The amount of charge in the blank is determined by how close the gun is going to be to its target when it is fired. The closer the gun, the smaller the charge in the blank.

A weapons master is always on the set when actors are going to use guns, and the safety of everyone is the weapons master's responsibility. If an actor has never shot a gun before, or has little experience with the gun he or she is going to use, the weapons master will take the actor to a shooting range for training in gun safety. The weapons master is present when the scene is filmed, and as soon as the director yells "Cut!" the weapons master

calls, "Finger off the trigger; weapon down." The actor points the gun's barrel to the ground and waits until the weapons master removes it from his or her hand.

All these safety precautions usually keep actors from being hurt, but when movie audiences see a gun battle on screen the gunshots look very real—thanks to something called a squib. A squib, sometimes called a bullet hit, is a tiny smokeless explosive charge mounted onto a grooved metal plate, which is backed by a piece of leather to protect the actor's skin. The squib is concealed under the actor's clothing. A small bag of fake blood is usually mounted next to the charge. If the shot is going to be very gory, butcher's scraps may be included in the blood bag and the squib may be covered with a thin piece of latex made to resemble the actor's skin. A concealed wire runs from the detonating cap on the squib to a place out of camera range, where it is set off electrically by the weapons master on the set. A real bullet will tear clothing, so in order to get the right effect from a squib, the actor's clothing must be carefully prepared either by light scoring with a knife or sanding. "We just do something to break the fabric down before the charge goes off," says Gabe Videla. "But the clothing is still intact before the shot. You can't see what we've done."

When the director calls "Action!" and the gunfire goes off, a special effects technician who holds a license to handle gunpowder uses a battery to detonate the squib. *Pow!* The clothing rips, blood spurts, and the actor groans (or dies) until the director yells "Cut!"

A close-up look at various bullet hits, or squibs *(left)*. At Special Effects Unlimited, Bob Willard attaches the bullet hits to detonating wires *(right)*.

In truly violent scenes actors are sometimes fitted with dozens of squibs all over their bodies. This is how they filmed actress Faye Dunaway's "death" in the 1967 film *Bonnie and Clyde*. Even the car was peppered with "bullets." To achieve that effect, holes were drilled into the car's body and a squib with the proper charge was put in each hole. Then the holes were plugged up and painted over. When the right moment came, the squibs were detonated and the plugs blew out. It looked as if the car, too, was being riddled by bullets.

Not only do gunshot wounds have to look real, the weapons that fire them must be appropriate. You cannot use an 1887 lever-action shotgun for a movie about the Civil War. Even the earliest moviemakers realized the necessity of having historical weapons to use in the movies. Cecil B. DeMille teamed up with James Sydney Stembridge to collect movie weapons. Today the Stembridge Gun Collection, run by James's nephew, Syd, is the largest in the world, and it provides many historical weapons to moviemakers. The people at Stembridge were asked to create the special shotgun that Arnold Schwarzenegger used in *Terminator 2*. They modified an 1887 shotgun in their collection, cutting it down and balancing it so the actor could wield it in a way that made it look like a futuristic weapon rather than the antique that it was.

For safety's sake, the fewer guns that are capable of firing on a movie set, the better. Joe Lombardi has real guns, but he also has a large collection of rubber ones that would fool anyone who did not know better. The rubber guns are carefully weighted. It is important that the guns *feel* real, so the actors will carry them properly.

Knives, or edged weapons, as they are occasionally called in the movie business, are treated as carefully as guns on a movie set, because knives can be just as dangerous. As with firearms, a weapons master is always in charge of them. If a scene calls for a stabbing, a blood knife will be used. Blood knives are real knives with surgical tubing attached to the back. Depending on the kind of wound needed—stab or slice—the tube will be attached to the edge or the tip of the knife. Movie blood is squeezed into the surgical tube, and the actor using the knife controls when and how the blood is released as the knife finds its mark.

Like smoke, blood can also be created by using chemicals. This method is often used for a knife wound. One chemical is spread on the dull edge of the knife and the other is placed on the actor's skin. Where the blade makes contact with the skin and the two chemicals react, a thin streak of "blood" appears.

Joe Lombardi's company also makes props, short for properties. A prop is any article used in a movie other than costumes and scenery. Most props are the real thing—a real broom, a real china vase, a real tube of toothpaste. However, there are films that call for break-

Joe Lombardi poses with a Bowie blood knife *(top)*. When Joe squeezes the handle of the knife, fake blood is forced out of small holes at the tip of the blade *(bottom)*.

away props. Breakaways are used in a film when things need to break easily—and painlessly, if an actor is involved. Westerns, especially older ones, frequently show chairs getting broken over someone's head. That kind of chair is made of balsa wood or Styrofoam that has been glued, not nailed, together. On any given day at Special Effects Unlimited one might see an assortment of delicate figurines and ornaments, glasses, dishes, chairs, bricks, or rocks that look as real as anything in your home or garden—but all of them are breakaways. Though breakaways technically are props rather than special effects, believable breakaways are often needed to complete an illusion.

In real life, getting smashed over the head with a chair or a plate would hurt, but if it happens in the movies with breakaways, it's more like a pillow fight. And audiences often wince at the haggard, bloody faces of "wounded" actors, but movie wounds can be fixed with soap and water instead of surgery and stitches.

Bob Willard pulls a breakaway parrot from its mold. When the parrot is painted and finished, it will look like a fine sculpture, but it could be crushed in one hand.

Ken Ralston and his 1/4–scale miniature train from *Back to the Future Part III*.

Miniatures in Motion

Miniatures have been used in the movies ever since Edwin S. Porter's movie *The Great Train Robbery,* an eleven-minute film that was released in 1903 and is sometimes described as the first story film. Porter did not have a camera capable of filming a full real train at once, so he used a toy train. Miniatures, or models, are still used today in filmmaking when, as George Lucas has said, "reality is too tough to deal with." For example, Ken Ralston used 1/4-scale miniatures for the car/train crash in *Back to the Future Part III.* Small replicas of the real thing substitute nicely when directors need to blow up buildings, sink boats, or do anything else that would be too dangerous, too expensive, or just plain impossible to film.

The 1982 film *Poltergeist* tells a frightening story of a haunted house that is finally destroyed by implosion. However, the screenplay just said, "And the house implodes." What an imploding house might look like, and how to create the effect, was left to the creative minds at ILM.

It is much more practical to wreck a 1/4-scale train than a real one! Here is the train wreck from *Back to the Future Part III.*

Richard Edlund is now the head of Boss Films, another famous special effects company, but he worked for ILM at the time *Poltergeist* was made. He was the FX supervisor on the film, and he planned the implosion. The special effects team built a miniature house, six feet by four feet, that was an exact replica of the real suburban tract house the filmmakers were using, right down to the pictures on the walls and the furniture in the rooms.

Wires were attached to every wall, window, and object in it. The wires were designed to pull everything down into a high-suction funnel underneath the table the model sat on. Just to be certain that the house would *really* collapse when the time came, two men with pump shotguns stood by, ready to fire into it as it was sucked into the funnel.

The special effects artists knew that it would take only five seconds to pull the house and its contents into the funnel—action that would take just a blink of an eye on-screen. The shot needed to last longer, so everyone in the movie audience could enjoy the effect. In order to make the effect last longer, Richard Edlund decided to use one of the oldest special effects techniques in the movies—slow motion.

It may seem odd, but the faster the film runs through the movie camera, the slower the action appears on the screen. The slower the film goes through the camera, the faster the action appears on the screen. In early movies the cameras were slowly cranked by hand, which is why the action looks so fast. Today's movies are usually

No one would guess the imploding house in *Poltergeist* was actually a miniature.

filmed—and always projected—at 24 frames per second. However, for the imploding house, the film raced through the camera at the speed of 360 frames per second. Filming at this speed meant there were a lot more frames per second of action to project onto the movie screen, so the house imploded for many more seconds on-screen than it did in real time. The imploding house in *Poltergeist* took weeks to plan and five seconds to film, and cost $250,000 to create.

The people at ILM have a tradition of presenting at

The miniature mansion from *Death Becomes Her* would make a fabulous, though expensive, dollhouse.

least one model from a picture to the film's director. After the house imploded in *Poltergeist,* technicians scurried around and swept up all of the pieces. They sealed them into a lovely plastic box and presented it to Steven Spielberg, who—it is said—proudly displayed it on his piano.

The miniature train and car that were built for *Back to the Future* and the mansion that was created for *Death Becomes Her* may look like fabulous toys, but in reality they were works of art before being, as miniatures often are, destroyed for an effect. Sometimes, however, a particular miniature will be saved. In 1979, several years before

Poltergeist, Steven Spielberg directed a motion picture called *1941.* Set during World War II, the film tells the story of panicked Los Angeles residents who are fearful that a Japanese submarine is going to attack the city. Greg Jein built the miniatures for that film, including a faithful duplication of the Pacific Coast Amusement Park. All of the attractions were there, including the Ferris wheel and a brightly lit, exquisitely detailed carousel, complete with hand-painted horses. Steven Spielberg saw the miniature set and fell in love with the carousel. However, the script called for the park to be destroyed by shelling from the submarine (also a miniature). Spielberg could not bear the thought of crushing the carousel. As the director, he had the right to change the shot, and he did. The Ferris wheel was destroyed and rolled off the end of the miniature dock, but the tiny carousel was spared.

The Hunt for Red October is a movie about 650-foot-long nuclear submarines. Since governments take a dim view of lending out their *real* nuclear subs to a movie company, the producers had to use miniatures, and they asked the model makers at Industrial Light and Magic to make them. The detailed models looked identical to the real things, but they ranged in size from six feet to twenty-two feet—quite a bit smaller than their real-life counterparts! The models were wonderful, but the movie's director, John McTiernan, had a serious problem. "At three hundred feet below sea level," he says, "there is no light; it's pitch-black. That was the tricky part." Indeed it was tricky. No one wants to watch a black submarine slide through black water, no matter how accurate it is. We need some light to see things. The magicians at ILM decided that most audiences would not really *know* what the water looked like three hundred feet below the surface, so they decided to create a scene that would seem right even though, technically, it was incorrect.

The models of the submarines were attached to specially constructed wire rigging and suspended over the set. In order to simulate the ocean's depths, smoke was blown over everything. When the director was ready to shoot the scene, a computer attached to the models' rigging moved the entire apparatus in a preprogrammed plan called go motion, a refinement of the more traditional stop-motion animation.

Even though a motion picture camera exposes only one frame at a time, the film is constantly moving through the camera. In live-action photography, the actors and/or animals are also constantly moving. The effect of the moving film, coupled with the moving actors, creates a kind of blurring between the frames. Traditional stop-motion animation cannot capture this blurring motion—it isn't there, because the object is inanimate and is perfectly still all the time. Go motion is part of a motion control system that allows the computer to move the models at a constant rate of speed as the camera films them. This steady movement of inanimate objects causes the slight, but important, realistic blur between the frames of film.

The go-motion process was used in 1982 to animate both a miniature and a full-sized puppet of E.T. in the film

Miniature submarines are filmed with the go–motion process for *The Hunt for Red October.*

E.T. The Extra-Terrestrial. The following year a miniature forest was created for some scenes in *Return of the Jedi,* and the go-motion process was used again. The miniatures and the motion techniques in films like *E.T., Return of the Jedi,* and *Death Becomes Her* all contributed to Dennis Muren's and Ken Ralston's winning Academy Awards for special effects for their work on these films.

For some scenes in *Return of the Jedi,* the real redwood forest was duplicated in miniature.

Dennis Muren poses in front of a matte painting of Los Angeles. E.T. sits in the foreground.

Mattes and Plates

A frame of movie film is composed of many different elements, including the actors, the background, and the sound. When all these elements are filmed together, moviemakers say they have shot the scene in camera. For years, that was the *only* way movies were made. No one knew how to separate the different parts, then reassemble them to achieve a desired effect. However, as technology has improved, filmmakers have been able to achieve fantastic visual effects by combining separate elements into one finished shot.

Earthquake is an early-1970s disaster film about an earthquake that hits the city of Los Angeles. There is a scene in the film that shows hundreds of people fleeing from the Ahmanson Theater in the Los Angeles Music Center as the quake occurs. No one was going to destroy the real theater, of course, so a perfectly scaled model was constructed. Next, the Universal Studio filmmakers made an establishing shot, which portrays the basic situation in any scene. Several hundred extras (actors who have no lines in a movie) were filmed running in a panic out of the real Ahmanson Theater in downtown Los Angeles, as if a real quake was occurring. When that shot was completed, the cameraman noted the position and angle of the camera and, back in the studio, duplicated it exactly in relation to the model theater. Then the camera crew filmed the model theater getting shaken apart. At the appropriate place, the two pieces of film were joined together. As a result of this bit of trickery, the audience sees a realistic scene of people pouring from the real theater; then the film cuts to a scene of the model theater getting destroyed. This second scene works because no actors were in the scene with the model—real people towering over a model would of course destroy the illusion.

There are times, however, when models won't work, because actors must be in the scene. For example, there is a famous scene in the 1983 film *Return of the Jedi* in which Princess Leia rides an airborne bike through a dense redwood forest at breakneck speed. FX supervisors Dennis Muren, Ken Ralston, and Richard Edlund could not have used a forest of model trees for that kind of shot. Actress Carrie Fisher, who played the part of the princess, would have dwarfed them. A real forest was needed, and real actors had to fly through it on speeder bikes. Impossible, you say? Not with something called a bluescreen.

The bluescreen is just that—an illuminated blue screen. It is often used for flying effects, such as Princess Leia's ride through the forest, the children's flying bikes in *E.T.,* and the floating feather in *Forrest Gump*. For *Return of the Jedi,* Carrie Fisher rode the bike in front of a bluescreen in an ILM studio. She never came near a forest. When the bluescreen film was processed (in a special way), there were two shots. One was of Princess Leia riding her bike against a black background, and the other was of Princess Leia's silhouette, in black, against a white background. Both shots are called traveling mattes. *Matte* is a French word meaning "mask"; in film, mattes are used to mask off areas of light, preventing portions of the frame from being exposed. Traveling mattes work in the same way, but change shape from frame to frame.

Once the FX supervisors had the proper traveling mattes, the princess had to be placed in the forest. The FX supervisors needed a background plate—film of a real redwood forest. When Dennis Muren had decided on the proper forest, cameraman Garrett Brown used a camera called a Steadicam. The Steadicam was mounted on a rig that Garrett Brown wore on his body. The rig steadied the camera, allowing Garrett to take smooth, even footage of the woods as he walked through, filming the background plate. But Princess Leia's bike ride appears to be done at breakneck speed. The redwood trees fly by her. The illusion of speed was achieved by having Garrett walk through the woods filming at a very slow frame-per-second rate. Remember, the slower the film goes through the camera, the faster the action appears on the screen when the film is projected. The result of this effort was a background plate of trees whizzing by the camera.

Carrie Fisher as Princess Leia rides a bike in front of a bluescreen.

So now the wizards at ILM had three elements: the background plate and two traveling mattes—one of Princess Leia in black silhouette and the other of her riding her bike. Putting them together, however, was a complicated process. You might think that the effect could be achieved by simply rephotographing the bluescreen film of the actress against the background of the forest. It isn't that simple, because film is transparent.

Suppose you had two snapshot negatives, one of yourself and one of your brother. As a trick, you want to paste your face onto your brother's body. You could carefully cut your face from your negative and paste it over your

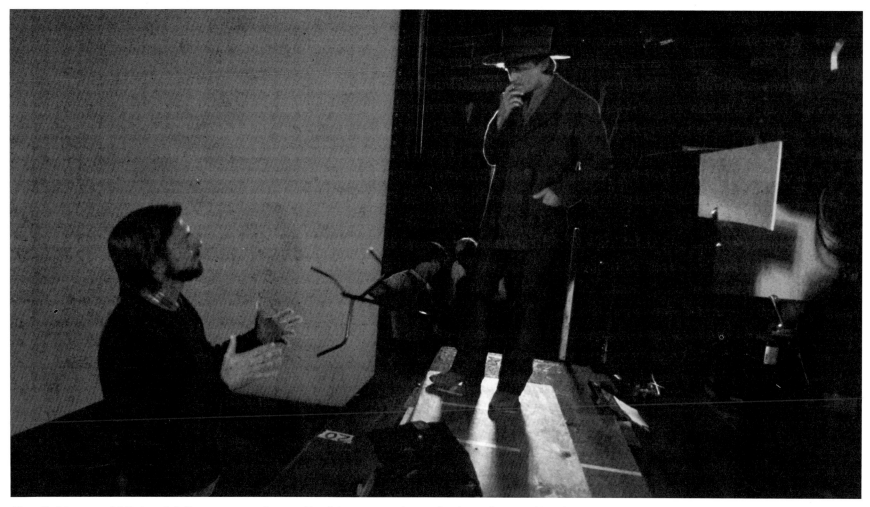

Ken Ralston and Michael J. Fox prepare to use the bluescreen to make traveling mattes for a scene in *Back to the Future Part III*.

brother's face. But the trick wouldn't work because of the film's transparency. Your brother's face would show beneath yours. For your trick to work, you would need something to mask out your brother's face before you replaced it with your own. It is the same in moviemaking.

If the forest and the princess had been put together without using the mattes that were created in the bluescreen process, Princess Leia would have been double-exposed. The viewer would have seen the forest right through her, which would have spoiled the illusion.

To prevent that from happening, the traveling matte of her silhouette was photographed against the background scene. Then there was a piece of film of the woods and a nice black spot in the exact shape of the princess on her bike that masked out the forest background. The color film of the princess on her bike was lined up *precisely* over the black matte of her image and the entire film "sandwich" was reshot. Abracadabra! The resulting illusion shows her speeding through a forest she never, in reality, entered.

That's the way a matte is created photographically. Mattes can also be painted, and no discussion of special effects would be complete without reference to matte paintings and the artists who create them.

Matte paintings are used to replace or change part of an image. Jesse Silver is a matte artist who began as a fine artist—someone who sold his paintings to collectors. Jesse says, "I got into this business because I wanted to try something different and challenging."

Creating matte paintings for the movies is a different kind of challenge from that of creating landscapes to hang on the walls of homes, offices, or museums. However, the quality of the paintings is the same. A matte artist must be able to paint a scene with such realism that it looks like a photograph. Jesse Silver is able to do this, and his talent has been used by FX supervisors on many different projects, from *Coneheads* to *Lonesome Dove.*

Lonesome Dove was filmed in New Mexico in the late spring. However, the producers wanted to show the ranch in winter, and they didn't want to wait for winter to arrive. The FX supervisor turned to Jesse and asked him to do a matte painting.

"I went to Angel Fire, New Mexico, the location where they were filming," Jesse says. "I took my paints and my glass, trudged out to the location in the middle of *nowhere,* set up the camera, and bolted it in place. Then I looked through the viewfinder at the ranch house scene in the distance. There was the house, and the fence surrounding it."

Next, Jesse set up the large piece of glass in a sturdy frame in front of the camera, and he began to paint. He painstakingly duplicated exactly what the camera was seeing—with one difference: He added snow to the roof of the house, the ground around the ranch, and the tops of the fence posts. The crew was in a hurry to complete the shot before stormy weather moved in, and Jesse painted through the night, finishing just before seven-thirty in the morning, when the film crew arrived. The crew took three shots of the ranch in Jesse Silver's painted "winter," pulled the glass away from in front of the camera, and proceeded to shoot the ranch in springtime. They had their background plates of the ranch in the spring and in "winter," and they finished just before the storm moved in.

Back in California, they would use these plates combined with live-action shots to put together the final composited print of the scene. A composited shot is a picture that is put together in layers—a kind of celluloid sandwich that allows filmmakers to create scenes that are

A matte artist at ILM works on a glass painting for *Die Hard 2*.

either impractical or impossible to film in real life. There is an art to putting the layers together, and even the best special effects artists can make mistakes.

In the film *Raiders of the Lost Ark,* the final scene is a shot of a warehouse, which is really a matte painting with a trapezoidal shape left clear. The actor playing the warehouse man was photographed through this piece of clear glass. However, sharp-eyed viewers can see the top of the actor's head vanishing behind the edge of the matte painting. Apparently, when the scene was put together, everything was not lined up as precisely as it should have been.

The famous imploded house from *Poltergeist* is also an optically composited shot. One element in that shot is footage of the model house imploding. Another element is the background plate of the actual neighborhood in southern California where the real house was located. A third element is a matte painting of the neighborhood; in the painting, the sky is an eerie gray color. Finally there are lightning effects that were created back in the studio. It took four different elements, composited together, to create the horrifying imploding house.

Bluescreen work, background plates, matte paintings—these are all optical tricks of the trade that filmmakers use to create movie magic.

At ILM, Geoff Campbell uses his computer to add finishing details to a *Jurassic Park* dinosaur.

Computers—The Magician's New Wand

Computers are changing the way we live, and computers are also changing the way Hollywood makes movies. Pictures, even snapshots, can now be scanned into a computer, turning the pictures into a digital image represented by a set of dots called pixels—short for picture elements. Once the conversion happens, anyone at the computer terminal can begin to manipulate the pixels, which is exactly what Kevin Yagher was doing when he stretched Ted Danson's and Macaulay Culkin's smiles all the way back to their ears. The computer image can then be transferred to film, just as you print something from your computer screen onto paper.

Kevin Yagher is only thirty-two years old and yet he says, "If I don't learn how to master this computer, I'll soon be a dinosaur." Kevin is referring to the future of special effects. According to many people, in the future all visual special effects will be done on a computer. In fact, the day may come when actors perform in a special blue room—a larger version of the bluescreen—and everything else is added by computer!

This new age of computer graphics, or CG, images really came into its own with the creation of the T-1000 cyborg in *Terminator 2: Judgment Day.* Who can forget the metallic creature who oozed up from the floor and changed smoothly and effortlessly into human form, then back into a blob? The cyborg was amazing, but the *Tyrannosaurus rex* of *Jurassic Park* soon edged *Terminator 2*'s cyborg out of the headlines. Both creatures had their beginnings at a computer workstation.

For *Jurassic Park,* Mark Dippe was a member of ILM's computer graphics team. At first, director Steven Spielberg had planned to use traditional models and animation for his film, but Mark Dippe was eager to try computer animation. He began to work secretly on his computer, creating dinosaur bones. When he had fashioned a complete skeleton of a *T. rex,* he animated it in a running motion and showed it to his supervisor, Dennis Muren. Dennis was impressed with Mark's work and showed it to Spielberg and the movie's producers. The result was a go-ahead to create the *T. rex* in the computer for use in all the scenes except those that were shot live with the actors.

The animators began with a casting of Stan Winston's 1/5-scale model of the *T. rex.* They took the model to a facility called Cyberware Laboratories, where it was sliced into sections that were then scanned into a computer. The eventual result was a three-dimensional wire-frame computer puppet of the *T. rex.* The *T. rex* could be manipulated like a puppet with an armature—only this time, the animation would be done with a mouse on a computer.

In order to animate a model by computer, some—but not all—of its positions are entered into the computer. Animators fill in the missing movements by a computer-assisted process called morphing, but they have to make constant adjustments for realism. In the case of *Jurassic Park* this was a problem, since no one knew exactly how dinosaurs moved. Everyone relied on Phil Tippett's performance bible, which choreographed all dinosaur movements. Steve Williams was the primary animator for a spectacular scene in the movie, in which the *T. rex* was supposed to chase a Jeep traveling at twenty miles per hour. "Some people argued that the *T. rex* never ran unless it had to, and if it ran, it would do so for a short period of time and move very fast," Steve says. "I had to throw logic out the window and create a *T. rex* that moved at sixty miles per hour, even though its hollow bones would probably have busted if he ran that fast. We had to invent a dinosaur and try to make it look believable."

Movement was not the only thing that made the *T. rex* believable. Other programs developed at ILM gave the CG dinosaur scales, dirt, shine, shadows, and skin wrinkles.

There are four basic steps to computer animation: modeling, animating, rendering, and compositing. You have read about modeling and animating. Creating the skin texture was part of the rendering process. At this point the creature in the computer is three-dimensional,

Computer wizardry enabled Forrest Gump to be shown talking to the late President John F. Kennedy *(left)*. Ken Ralston and Doug Chiang used computers to insert Tom Hanks's image into historical film footage *(right)*.

but film is two-dimensional, so the next step involves converting everything in the computer to a two-dimensional image compatible with film. And finally the finished creature, with its movements, is composited into a background plate in a manner that is similar to bluescreen work—but all done in the computer.

Computers can be used to make creatures that do not exist, and they can be used to put people in places they never were. *In the Line of Fire* is a movie about a Secret Service agent, played by Clint Eastwood, who is haunted by the fact that he was on duty when President John F. Kennedy was assassinated. There is only one piece of

authentic film taken of that terrible moment. It was shot by an amateur photographer named Abraham Zapruder. That piece of film has been shown thousands of times, and of course Clint Eastwood is not in it. Now, thanks to computer magic, Eastwood's face has been injected into the Zapruder film to add realism to *In the Line of Fire.*

Later, the same technique was refined even more. Ken Ralston was the FX supervisor for *Forrest Gump,* a film in which historical footage of deceased presidents Kennedy, Lyndon Johnson, and Richard Nixon was digitally manipulated to allow actor Tom Hanks to appear in several scenes with the presidents. Hanks is even shown carrying

Tom Hanks sat on a park bench while the background plate for a scene from *Forrest Gump* was shot, and then cameras filmed a nonexistent feather as if it were floating through the air.

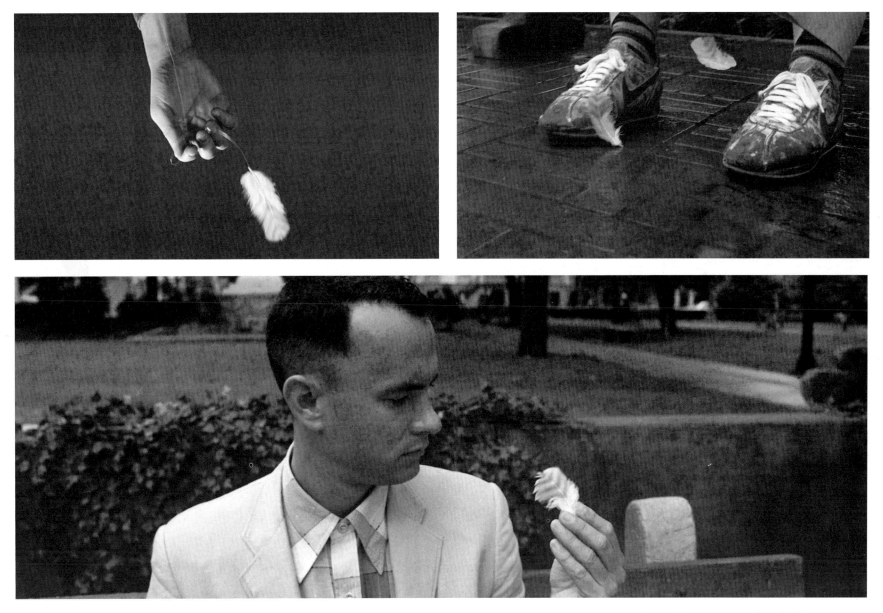

Back at ILM's studios, a turkey feather, attached to a thin line and blown by a fan, was filmed in front of a bluescreen *(top left)*. Computers were used to "erase" the image of the real feather attached to Hanks's shoe *(top right)*. At the end of the sequence, Hanks holds the floating feather *(bottom)*. The scene was on the screen for two minutes, but it took six months to produce.

on brief conversations with the presidents at the White House!

The floating-feather sequence in the opening of *Forrest Gump* was optically composited, too. First, background plates of Hanks sitting on a park bench with a real turkey feather glued to his shoe were shot. Then Ken Ralston filmed a nonexistent feather as if it were floating through the air and brushing against people and objects in the

Actor Gary Sinise prepares to lose his lower legs—thanks to bluescreen stockings that will enable them to be optically removed from each frame of film *(left)*. Sinise as he appears on–screen in *Forrest Gump (right)*.

park. That film was scanned into a computer at ILM. Back at the special effects facility, Ken attached a thin, clear line to a turkey feather, blew a fan on it, and filmed its movements against a bluescreen. Sometimes he used slow motion, running the camera at seventy-two frames per second. Artists working at computer stations gave the film of the floating feather shadows and other realistic touches as they layered the feather's flight on top of the background plate of the park. Because the background plate had some glimpses of the real feather attached to Hanks's shoe (when it was supposed to be floating), computers were used again to "erase" the stationary feather and replace it with a perfect match of the image of Hanks's shoe and the brickwork underneath it. The dance of the feather is on the screen for two minutes, but it took a computer running twenty-four hours a day for five days to generate the visual effects and six months to produce the final shot.

In another spectacular effect in that movie, computers "erased" the lower legs of actor Gary Sinise, making him a believable amputee. To accomplish this effect, the lower parts of Sinise's legs were fitted with bluescreen stockings, which were then optically removed from each frame of film. Steven Rosenbaum is the computer graphics supervisor who did that work, and he says, "There is no doubt from the audience that Gary Sinise is an amputee."

Computers are the magic wand of the special effects future. Will computers turn model makers, matte painters, makeup artists, and stunt actors into dinosaurs of the film world? That's not likely to happen. Jesse Silver is painting his mattes on computers now, but it is still *he* who is the artist. Kevin Yagher can use a computer to create a funny makeup effect, but it is still Kevin, not the computer, deciding what is funny. People will need to conceive of the special effects that add magic to movies, others will need to design them, still others will need to write the programs that execute them. Ken Ralston says, "Computer-generated effects are an amazing tool, but that is all they are—a tool. They are only as good as the artists who do this work. And the effects should only be there to serve the story. *Gone With the Wind* was a tremendous effects film, but no one noticed that because the film told a story about the human condition. Storytelling is at the heart of filmmaking."

Author's Note

Safety precautions are always taken on the sets of movies. However, there have been incidents—such as Brandon Lee's fatal shooting with a gun that was supposed to contain blanks, during filming of *The Crow,* and the helicopter crash that killed Vic Morrow and two young children, My-Ca Le and Renee Chen, during filming of *Twilight Zone: The Movie*—that are true tragedies. No discussion of special effects work would be complete without mentioning those sad events. Effects involving knives, guns, or gunpowder are strictly regulated by law, require a license, and must *never* be attempted by anyone who is not a professional.

Afterword

The Academy Awards, or Oscars, are the highest honors the Academy of Motion Picture Arts and Sciences can bestow upon filmmakers. Following is a list of films that have won the Academy Award for Special Visual Effects throughout the years.

1927–28 *Wings*	1958 *Tom Thumb*	1977 *Star Wars*
1939 *The Rains Came*	1959 *Ben-Hur*	1978 *Superman*
1940 *The Thief of Bagdad*	1960 *The Time Machine*	1979 *Alien*
1941 *I Wanted Wings*	1961 *The Guns of Navarone*	1980 *The Empire Strikes Back*
1942 *Reap the Wild Wind*	1962 *The Longest Day*	1981 *Raiders of the Lost Ark*
1943 *Crash Dive*	1963 *Cleopatra*	1982 *E.T. The Extra-Terrestrial*
1944 *Thirty Seconds over Tokyo*	1964 *Mary Poppins*	1983 *Return of the Jedi*
1945 *Wonder Man*	1965 *Thunderball*	1984 *Indiana Jones and the*
1946 *Blithe Spirit*	1966 *Fantastic Voyage*	*Temple of Doom*
1947 *Green Dolphin Street*	1967 *Doctor Dolittle*	1985 *Cocoon*
1948 *Portrait of Jennie*	1968 *2001: A Space Odyssey*	1986 *Aliens*
1949 *Mighty Joe Young*	1969 *Marooned*	1987 *Innerspace*
1950 *Destination Moon*	1970 *Tora! Tora! Tora!*	1988 *Who Framed Roger Rabbit*
1951 *When Worlds Collide*	1971 *Bedknobs and Broomsticks*	1989 *The Abyss*
1952 *Plymouth Adventure*	1972 *The Poseidon Adventure*	1990 *Total Recall*
1953 *The War of the Worlds*	1973 No award	1991 *Terminator 2: Judgment Day*
1954 *20,000 Leagues Under the Sea*	1974 *Earthquake*	1992 *Death Becomes Her*
1956 *The Bridges at Toko-Ri*	1975 *The Hindenburg*	1993 *Jurassic Park*
1957 *The Enemy Below*	1976 *King Kong*	1994 *Forrest Gump*

Index

Photo Credits

Pages 8, 27 (right), 64, 66, 68, 70, 72, 76, 80, courtesy of ILM, a division of Lucas Digital Limited; copyright Universal City Studios, Inc.; courtesy of MCA Publishing Rights, a division of MCA Inc.; all rights reserved.

Pages 12, 14–17, 44, courtesy of Museum of Modern Art/Film Stills Archive.

Page 18, copyright 1933 RKO Pictures, Inc.; used by permission, Turner Entertainment Company.

Pages 19, 50, 54 (bottom), copyright 1939 Turner Entertainment Company; all rights reserved.

Pages 20, 71, 75, courtesy of Lucasfilm Ltd.; *Return of the Jedi,* trademark and copyright Lucasfilm Ltd. (LFL) 1983.

Page 22, courtesy of Lucasfilm Ltd.; *Star Wars,* trademark and copyright Lucasfilm Ltd. (LFL) 1977.

Page 23, courtesy of Lucasfilm Ltd.; *The Empire Strikes Back,* trademark and copyright Lucasfilm Ltd. (LFL) 1980.

Pages 25, 83–86, courtesy of ILM, a division of Lucas Digital Limited; trademark and copyright 1994 Paramount Pictures.

Pages 26, 36, courtesy of Stan Winston Studio; art by Mark "Crash" McCreery; copyright Universal City Studios, Inc.; courtesy of MCA Publishing Rights, a division of MCA Inc.; all rights reserved.

Pages 27 (left), 37–40, courtesy of Stan Winston Studio; copyright Universal City Studios, Inc.; courtesy of MCA Publishing Rights, a division of MCA Inc.; all rights reserved.

Pages 28, 30–34, 46–48, courtesy of Kevin Yagher Productions, Inc.

Page 35, courtesy of Stan Winston Studio.

Page 42, courtesy of Museum of Modern Art/Film Stills Archive; copyright Universal City Studios, Inc.; courtesy of MCA Publishing Rights, a division of MCA Inc.; all rights reserved.

Page 45, courtesy of Museum of Modern Art/Film Stills Archive; copyright 1967 Twentieth Century Fox Film Corporation and Apjac Productions, Inc.; all rights reserved.

Page 49, courtesy of the Academy of Motion Picture Arts and Sciences; copyright 1993 Twentieth Century Fox Film Corporation; all rights reserved.

Page 53, courtesy of the Academy of Motion Picture Arts and Sciences; copyright Universal City Studios, Inc.; courtesy of MCA Publishing Rights, a division of MCA Inc.; all rights reserved.

Page 54 (top), courtesy of Museum of Modern Art/Film Stills Archive; copyright 1952 Turner Entertainment Company; all rights reserved.

Pages 55, 61–63, courtesy of Special Effects Unlimited, Inc.

Page 56, courtesy of Special Effects Unlimited, Inc.; trademark and copyright 1991 Paramount Pictures.

Page 57, courtesy of the *Cleveland Plain Dealer.*